What Wondrous Love

DEVOTIONS FOR
THE HOME

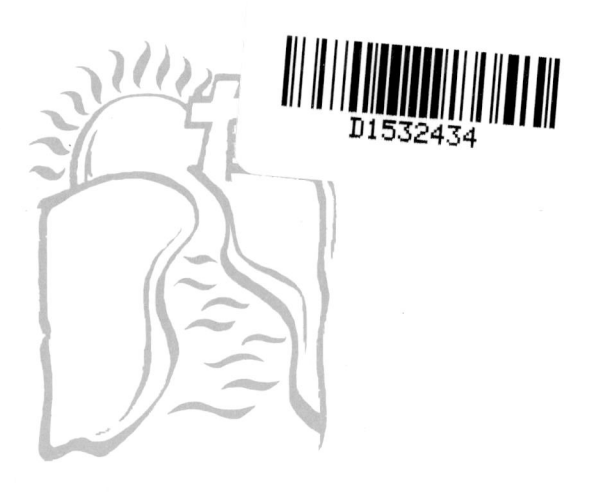

LENT

HOLY WEEK   EASTER

Meditations by Jay Cooper Rochelle
with
Household activities by Susan Palo Cherwien

Augsburg Fortress
Minneapolis

WHAT WONDROUS LOVE
Devotions for Lent, Holy Week, Easter

Scripture quotations, unless otherwise noted, are from the New Revised Standard Version Bible © 1989 Division of Christian Education of the National Council of the Churches of Christ in the U.S.A. Used by permission.

Revised Common Lectionary copyright © 1992 Consultation on Common Texts (CCT), 1522 K Street, NW, Suite 1000, Washington, DC 20005-1202. All rights reserved.

Blessings and prayers, unless otherwise noted, are newly-composed or from: *Welcome Home: Scripture, Prayers, and Blessings for the Household, Year of Matthew* copyright ©1995 Augsburg Fortress and *Welcome Home: Scripture, Prayers, and Blessings for the Household, Year of Mark* copyright © 1996 Augsburg Fortress.

Sources of hymns, poems, prayers, and other seasonal materials are acknowledged on pages 89–92.

Editors: Samuel Torvend, Linda Parriott
Cover design: Circus Design
Interior design: Marti Naughton
Interior art: Brian Jensen

Library of Congress Cataloging-in-Publication Data

Rochelle, Jay C.
   What wondrous love : devotions for Lent, Holy Week, Easter / Jay
Rochelle.
     p.   cm.
   Includes bibliographical references.
   ISBN 0-8066-2983-5 (alk. paper)
   1. Lent—Prayer-books and devotions—English. 2. Holy Week—Prayer-books and
devotions—English. 3. Easter—Prayer-books and devotions—English. I. Title.
BV85.R53   1996
242' .34—DC20
         96-44814
         CIP

Printed in the U.S.A.   ISBN 0-8066-2983-5   10-29835

02 01 00 99   2 3 4 5 6 7 8

Table of Contents

How to use this book

This book is filled with many signs that will lead the household on the path through Lent, Holy Week, and Easter. It can be used in different ways depending upon the schedules, circumstances, and needs of a particular home. Use whatever works well in your setting. Adapt what is presented here to your rhythm of life. Enrich the suggestions of this book with the prayers, customs, and songs that are cherished in your home.

Gathering for a brief daily or weekly prayer can take place in different settings. In some homes, people gather throughout the forty days of Lent by the light of a burning candle. During Holy Week, a family may gather around a cross or an image of the crucified Jesus. Throughout Easter's fifty days, some people will pray by a bowl of water, a vase of flowers, and the Easter candle. Wherever you gather for prayer, use the blessings, which may begin or be the center of your prayer.

In many homes with children, certain seasonal customs become cherished treasures that are handed on from one generation to another. This book includes *holiday customs* from around the world that set forth visually the meaning of the weekly and festival scripture readings. In addition, this book includes *prayers for young children.* Since many of the prayers are easily memorized, they can carry the meaning of the week or the season throughout each day. Many of the prayers are especially useful at bedtime.

Some people may want to use this book primarily as a source for scripture reading and reflection. To that end, a *meditation* has been included for each week and festival day. It is inspired by the *scripture readings* that are suggested for use throughout the week. In addition to the meditations, you will find a gathering of *poems;* some are quite old, while others are newly-composed. Each one serves as an artist's reflection of the season or the suggested scripture readings.

Over fifteen *songs* and *hymns* have been included in this book for use in the home. Some may be quite familiar to you. If this is so, sing them whenever you can. If you have other favorite hymns or songs, sing them, too. For those who do not sing, listen to a recording of Lenten and Easter songs or simply meditate on the hymn texts printed here. In the back of this book, the *index* lists many alternate tunes for singing with the printed text.

If your household is filled with so much activity that there are only a few times each week when everyone gathers for a meal, then be sure to use the *table prayer* printed for that week. These short prayers will set the meal within the larger context of the season and its unique interpretation of Christ's presence in the household. If time allows, have one person at the table read a brief portion of scripture or the appropriate prayer for the week.

One of the great gifts of this book is the invitation to use all the human senses. One can read, hear, sing, taste, touch, and see the presence of Christ in the home throughout the days of Lent, Holy Week, and Easter.

What wondrous love

This early American folk song is a great hymn of praise that uses ancient biblical images to speak of Christ who "laid aside his crown for my soul." Perhaps the unknown author of this hymn was inspired by the great hymn to Christ quoted by Paul in his letter to the Philippians: "Though he was in the form of God . . . he emptied himself, taking the form of a slave . . . and became obedient unto death—even death on a cross" (2:5, 8). Both the American folk song and Paul's hymn are sung during the central season of the Christian year of grace. This is not surprising, for these two hymns summarize the center of Christian faith: Christ has died. Christ is risen. Christ will come again. It is this great mystery that Christians celebrate every Sunday and during the days of Lent, Holy Week, and Easter.

Lent is a forty-day journey to Easter. Christians keep company with Noah and his family who were in the ark for forty days, with the Hebrews who journeyed through the desert for forty years, and with Moses, Elijah, and Jesus who fasted for forty days before they embarked on the tasks God had prepared for them. During Lent, Christians journey with those who are preparing for baptism at Easter. Together, Christians reflect on the meaning of their baptismal promises. At the same time, the disciples of the Lord Jesus consider everything that leads away from love of God and neighbor. Fasting, prayer, and works of love—the discipline of Lent—help the household turn toward the gifts of baptism: God's forgiveness and healing.

During the final days of Holy Week, Christians celebrate the Lord's passion, death, and resurrection. In public worship, Christians celebrate the washing of feet and the Lord's Supper on Maundy

Thursday, the victory of the cross on Good Friday, the presence of God's light and salvation in the risen Christ on Holy Saturday and Easter Sunday. The ancient Christian name for the Three Days is the paschal feast, *paschal* referring to Jesus' "pasch" or passover from death to risen life. As the sun sets on Maundy Thursday, so Lent ends, and the Three Days begin, ending with sunset on Easter Day. During these central days, Christians prepare to celebrate God's gift of new life given in baptism. Indeed, the readings of the Three Days move us toward the baptismal font where new brothers and sisters are born of water and the Spirit, and where the baptized renew their baptismal promises.

The Three Days flow into the Fifty Days of Easter rejoicing. During this "week of weeks" Christians explore the meaning of the central actions of baptism for daily life: renouncing evil and professing one's faith, washing in water, being marked with the cross, clothing in the white robe, receiving the light of the paschal/Easter candle, and eating and drinking the bread of life and the cup of salvation. The entire Fifty Days were once called *Pentecost,* Greek for fifty. On the fiftieth day of Easter, Christians celebrate the mystery of the risen Christ sending the breath, wind, and fire of the Holy Spirit. With Paul and the unknown hymn writer, the household of faith joins a great throng of people throughout the world in singing to "God and the Lamb who is the great I AM." Lent brings us to Easter and Easter leads us from the grave to paradise.

Lent

Even now, says the Lord,
return to me with all your heart.

JOEL 2:12

Ash Wednesday

Return to the Lord, your God,
for he is gracious and merciful,
slow to anger, and abounding in steadfast love.

JOEL 2:13

Today we begin the Lenten journey. As we did at our baptism, we receive the sign of the cross on our foreheads. Marked again with the cross of Christ, we turn to the baptismal promises God has made to us, those promises that we affirm for ourselves. We ask again, What does it mean to be dust? What does it mean that to dust we shall return? Are we only this—nameless, shapeless ashes? Or can we claim these ashes as ours and recognize that though they speak the truth of our mortality, they also are made in the sign of a cross, the sign of our salvation? With this cross, Christ has made us his own forever. We know the end—we are claimed, marked, promised.

We have been baptized in the great sea of God's mercy. On this day, marked with ashen crosses, we join our brothers and sisters in the faith in order to hear God calling us away from death and into life. In the midst of a troubled world, we call out to God who is already with us, leading and nourishing us with wondrous love.

Sometimes I wake, and, lo, I have forgot,
And drifted out upon an ebbing sea!
My soul that was at rest now resteth not,
For I am with myself and not with thee;
Truth seems a blind moon in a glaring morn,
Where nothing is but sick-hearted vanity:
O, thou who knowest, save thy child forlorn.

GEORGE MACDONALD

HYMN

Savior, when in dust to you
low we bow in homage due;
when, repentant, to the skies
scarce we lift our weeping eyes;
oh, by all your pains and woe
suffered once for us below,
bending from your throne on high,
hear our penitential cry!

Tune: ABERSTWYTH—*other tunes are noted in the index*

FOR READING THROUGHOUT THE WEEK

Joel 2:1–17   Psalm 51
2 Corinthians 5:20—6:20   Matthew 6:1–21

A PRAYER FOR THE WEEK

Merciful God,
you do not despise sinners, but call us to repentance.
Wash us anew in the great waters of your mercy
and feed us on the bread of forgiveness. Amen

TABLE PRAYER

Two things, dear God, we need,
we ask them from your hand:
give us our daily bread;
forgive us all our sin. Amen

PRAYER WITH CHILDREN

Search me, O God, and know my heart;
test me and know my thoughts. Amen

see PSALM 139:23

FASTING FOR THE EYES

It has been said that there are three basic elements to the discipline of
the Lenten season: fasting for the good of the body, prayer for the
good of the soul, almsgiving or works of love for the good of
neighbor. An aspect of fasting is the simplification of our daily living.
This includes a heightened austerity in our surroundings, including
the veiling of crosses and religious images with purple cotton cloth or
simple unbleached muslin, thus creating a Lenten "fast for the eyes."

The First Week in Lent

Jesus fasted forty days and forty nights.
MATTHEW 4:2

Lent comes upon us, each year, as a shock. We can get used to the familiarity of God in the seasons of Christmas and Epiphany. Everyone loves little children, and that seems to be what those seasons are about, when you don't look too closely. Now comes Lent, a very different time.

It's easy to become distracted by sentiment and by the array of "stuff" associated with Christmas and Epiphany. Lent calls us to pay attention to God once again.

In the wilderness, the Evil One tried to distract Jesus, saying in effect, "Forget about God; try out this idea of being the messiah!" Jesus is not distracted. To each temptation he gives a response that more firmly plants him in the presence of God. Satan's test is based on making humans think that we have to grab all the good things for ourselves. Jesus knows that the good things are given to us so that we can, in turn, give them away. As Jesus says of himself, "the Son of Man came not to be served but to serve and to give his life a ransom for many."

In Lent, we are called, like Christ, to relocate ourselves in the presence and the will of God. We call this repentance: to change your mind, to re-orient your life, to follow God's will rather than your own. Follow Jesus on your lenten journey and learn the meaning of repentance, for only so shall we understand the wondrous love of God.

To you, O Lord, I lift up my soul.
O my God, in you I trust;
> *do not let me be put to shame;*
> *do not let my enemies exult over me.*
Do not let those who wait for you be put to shame;
> *let them be ashamed who are wantonly treacherous.*

Make me know your ways, O Lord;
> *teach me your paths.*
Lead me in your truth, and teach me,
> *for you are the God of my salvation;*
> *for you I wait all day long.*

Be mindful of your mercy, O Lord, and of your steadfast love,
> *for they have been from of old.*
Do not remember the sins of my youth or my transgressions;
> *according to your steadfast love remember me,*
> *for your goodness' sake, O Lord!*

PSALM 25:1-7

HYMN

A mighty fortress is our God, a sword and shield victorious;
he breaks the cruel oppressor's rod and wins salvation glorious.
The old satanic foe has sworn to work us woe!
With craft and dreadful might he arms himself to fight.
On earth he has no equal.

No strength of ours can match his might! We would be lost, rejected.
But now a champion comes to fight, whom God himself elected.
You ask who this may be? The Lord of hosts is he!
Christ Jesus, mighty Lord, God's only Son, adored.
He holds the field victorious.

Tune: EIN FESTE BERG

FOR READING THROUGHOUT THE WEEK

Genesis 2:15—3:7   Matthew 4:1–11
Genesis 9:8–17   Mark 1:9–15
Deuteronomy 26:1–11 Luke 4:1–13

A PRAYER FOR THE WEEK

Lord Jesus Christ,
in the desert you prepared to proclaim the reign of God.
In these forty days, lead us to live and proclaim God's reign. Amen

TABLE PRAYER

Lord our God,
as you fed our ancestors in the desert,
so now strengthen us with these gifts of food and drink.
Grant us life, sustain us, and help us in the days ahead. Amen

PRAYER WITH CHILDREN

Use this prayer at bedtime.

We give thanks to you, heavenly Father,
through Jesus Christ your Son,
that you have protected us this day.
Forgive us the wrong we have done.
Defend us from all dangers.
Send your holy angels to guard us. Amen

A PLACE FOR PRAYER

Set up a special place in the home for prayer during Lent. Clear away clutter; set down a simple cloth; and place a cross and, perhaps, a votive candle on the cloth. Use this as a quiet space for prayer, reflection, or meditation during the season.

BLESSING FOR A PLACE OF PRAYER

Blessed are you, O God of mercy and compassion.
Though we are but dust and ashes,
in baptism we die and rise with Christ.
As we ponder our sin and frailty,
assure us of your forgiveness and grace.
Nourish and sustain us on our Lenten journey,
that marked with the sign of the cross,
we may be brought to the promised land of Easter.
We make this prayer in the name of Jesus
who is Lord for ever and ever. Amen

The Second Week in Lent

As Moses lifted up the serpent in the wilderness,
so must the Son of Man be lifted up.

JOHN 3:14

Who is this Jesus? That seems to be the question that draws Nicodemus to Jesus one night. Nicodemus knew a lot about religion, and he apparently saw Jesus as a teacher who had a lot of interesting, exciting things to say about God. He realized that Jesus must be in the presence of God, but that was as far as he would let himself go.

Jesus wanted Nicodemus to move deeper. He wanted Nicodemus to see that there was more going on than teaching about God, more even than Jesus standing in the presence of God. Jesus invited Nicodemus to repent—simply to receive Jesus.

All of us have some of Nicodemus in us. We are attracted to Jesus for various reasons, and see him as someone worth listening to. But Jesus wants us, like Nicodemus, to move deeper, to be "born from above." During Lent, we are called to reorient ourselves toward God. We are invited to move beyond ideas about God, into a deeper relationship with God.

In his conversation with Nicodemus, Jesus refers to a time when the Israelites in the wilderness were beset by poisonous snakes. Those who were bitten needed only to look upon a bronze serpent which Moses lifted up on a staff and they would live. We are moving toward a time when we will see Jesus lifted up on the cross. All who look upon him in faith will live, and he will call us to himself in love. Even now, we are called beyond our initial ideas about Jesus, lifted to a height we had never imagined.

The same leaves over and over again!
They fall from giving shade above
To make one texture of faded brown
And fit the earth like a leather glove.

Before the leaves can mount again
To fill the trees with another shade,
They must go down past things coming up.
They must go down into the dark decayed.

They must *be pierced by flowers and put*
Beneath the feet of dancing flowers.
However it is in some other world
I know that this is the way in ours.

ROBERT FROST

HYMN

Baptized in water, sealed by the Spirit,
cleansed by the blood of Christ our king:
heirs of salvation, trusting his promise,
faithfully now God's praise we sing.

Baptized in water, sealed by the Spirit,
dead in the tomb with Christ our king:
one with his rising, freed and forgiven,
thankfully now God's praise we sing.

Tune: BUNESSAN *(Morning Has Broken)*

FOR READING THROUGHOUT THE WEEK

Genesis 12:1–4	John 3:1–17
Genesis 17:1–16	Mark 8:31–38
Genesis 15:1–18	Luke 13:31–35

A PRAYER FOR THE WEEK

O God,
you give your people power
to hope for that which is unseen.
Strengthen us so that we may follow your Son
with courage and humility. Amen

TABLE PRAYER

Hear us, O LORD,
as we offer you thanks for the gifts of this table.
Strengthen us on our journey with Christ,
your Son, who is our food and drink. Amen

PRAYER WITH CHILDREN

Use this prayer responsively.

The LORD says,
Do not fear,
I have called you by name, you are mine.
You have called me by name, dear God;
I am yours for ever. Amen

see ISAIAH 43:1

AS THE GRAIN OF WHEAT FALLS TO THE GROUND

Take a small container of potting soil and sprinkle wheat grass seeds
over the surface. Water gently and place in a sunny window.
Throughout the days of Lent you will see how the seeds change.
When they come together with water and sunlight, they are changed
from hard and dry to green and growing.

The Third Week in Lent

Those who drink of the water
that I will give them will never be thirsty.

JOHN 4:14

Jesus always gives us more than we think we are going to get. When Jesus met a Samaritan woman at a well, she was surprised that he even spoke to her—for Jews did not speak publicly to Samaritans. Just in his speaking to her, she received more than she would have expected. But that was only the beginning.

He asked for a drink of water, but in turn, Jesus gives water to those who thirst—to her and to us. The water he offers, though, is living water, the water of new life, of rebirth, and resurrection. This living water is given to us in our baptism, where we quench our spiritual thirst and enter a land flowing with milk and honey. Jesus' gift evokes Isaiah the prophet, who looked forward to a time when justice would roll down like water and righteousness like a flowing stream. Jesus brings this water, and more, to those among whom he ministers.

Still, Jesus wasn't done, because along with living water, Jesus gave the Samaritan woman a glimpse of a new way of living. He showed her that he knew her inside and out, laying bare all her faults. But he also shared with her—and only with her, in all of the gospel records—that he is the Messiah.

Jesus is himself the very reign of God, which he announces. When he includes those who are of the "wrong" gender or the "wrong" nation, he embodies the love and the compassion and the wholeness of God. In Christ, God steps over our boundaries to bring to all people more than they expect.

Your red blossoms amid green leaves
Are drooping, beautiful geranium!
But you do not ask for water.
You cannot speak! You do not need to speak—
Everyone knows that you are dying of thirst,
Yet they do not bring water!
They pass on, saying:
"The geranium wants water."
And I, who had happiness to share
And longed to share your happiness;
I who loved you, Spoon River,
And craved your love,
Withered before your eyes, Spoon River—
Thirsting, thirsting,
Voiceless from chasteness of soul to ask you for love,
You who knew and saw me perish before you,
Like this geranium which someone has planted over me,
And left to die.

EDGAR LEE MASTERS

HYMN

I heard the voice of Jesus say, "Come unto me and rest;
lay down, O weary one, lay down your head upon my breast."
I came to Jesus as I was, so weary, worn, and sad;
I found in him a resting place, and he has made me glad.

I heard the voice of Jesus say, "Behold, I freely give
the living water, thirsty one; stoop down and drink and live."
I came to Jesus, and I drank of that life-giving stream;
my thirst was quenched, my soul revived, and now I live in him.

Tune: KINGSFOLD—*other tunes are noted in the index*

FOR READING THROUGHOUT THE WEEK

Exodus 17:1–7   John 4:5–42
Exodus 20:1–17   John 2:13–22
Isaiah 55:1–9   Luke 13:1–9

A PRAYER FOR THE WEEK

O God,
we thirst for the water of life.
In your mercy, refresh us with the life-giving streams
of your word and holy supper. Amen

TABLE PRAYER

The LORD says:
All you who thirst, come to the waters;
and you that have no money, come eat and drink!
Listen carefully to me, and eat what is good. Amen

see ISAIAH 55:1, 2

PRAYER WITH CHILDREN

Now the day is over;
night is drawing nigh;
shadows of the evening
steal across the sky.

Jesus, give the weary
calm and sweet repose;
with your tend'rest blessing
may our eyelids close.

When the morning wakens,
then may I arise
pure and fresh and sinless
in your holy eyes.

THE SIGN OF THE CROSS

Lent is a fitting time to consider making the sign of the cross in prayer. God made us and loves us: our bodies, minds, and spirits. It is right that we worship God and pray with our whole being. Making the sign of the cross with hand upon body is a good place to begin involving the whole body in prayer. Place the thumb of the right hand against the tips of the first two fingers of the same hand. Touch your forehead, your heart, your left shoulder, then your right shoulder. To make this act a more tangible sign of your baptism, before making the sign of the cross, dip the group of three fingers into a bowl of fresh water kept at your prayer space.

THANKSGIVING FOR THE CROSS

Use this blessing at a place for prayer with a cross or image of the crucified Lord.

God our creator,
in the death of your Son,
you reveal your love for the whole creation.
Sealed with the sign of the cross,
you have claimed us as your children in holy baptism.
In these Forty Days,
lead us in our journey by the light of the holy cross
until we come to the joy of Easter's Fifty Days.
Grant this through Christ our Lord. Amen

The Fourth Week in Lent

I am the light of the world.

JOHN 9:5

Imagine the story of Jesus healing the blind man in John 9 as an overlay with one transparency placed atop another, as in anatomy textbooks or with some maps. On one layer we see a picture of physical blindness; Jesus heals this blindness for this one person. But looking through the physical need for healing, we see a need—our need—for healing which is spiritual, and which is the mission of Jesus throughout the gospel.

A man is healed, and religious leaders are shown to be blind to God's work in the world. This challenges us to consider our own blindness, "religious" though we may be. Then, too, notice that Christ heals the blind man, in part, through holding him up as a person of worth in his community. This calls us to repent, to rethink the place of all people in God's domain whom we cast out or cast aside. In healing the blind man, Jesus proclaims that God is at work to create and restore relationships so that people might become whole.

The questioners in the story don't get it. Their ideas of healing, sin, and sickness will not allow them to see what's going on. The story leads them and us forward, step by step. Eventually, we who were blind see—we are not called to analyze what has happened in the past, which is where the disciples begin in their conversation with Jesus. We are called to see what's happening in the present: the blind now see; the gospel is proclaimed.

I met a seer.
He held in his hands
The book of wisdom.
"Sir," I addressed him,
"Let me read."
"Child—" he began.
"Sir," I said,
"Think not that I am a child,
For already I know much
Of that which you hold.
Aye, much."

He smiled.
Then he opened the book
And held it before me.—
Strange that I should have grown so suddenly blind.

STEPHEN CRANE

HYMN

Amazing grace, how sweet the sound,
that saved a wretch like me!
I once was lost, but now am found;
was blind, but now I see.

'Twas grace that taught my heart to fear,
and grace my fears relieved;
how precious did that grace appear
the hour I first believed!

Tune: NEW BRITAIN

FOR READING THROUGHOUT THE WEEK

1 Samuel 16:1–13   John 9:1–41
Numbers 21:4–9   John 3:14–21
Joshua 5:9–12   Luke 15

A PRAYER FOR THE WEEK

Gracious God,
in your love you gave the world your Son.
Give us clear vision
so that we may see your grace and love
alive in this world and its people. Amen

TABLE PRAYER

We thank you, our creator,
for all things bright and good,
the seed-time and the harvest,
our life, our health, our food.
No gifts have we to offer
for all your love imparts,
but what you most would treasure—
our humble, thankful hearts. Amen

PRAYER WITH CHILDREN

Loving God, who gives us all things,
Grant, I pray, your child's request:
Guard my life throughout night's passing,
Help me gently, surely, rest.

From your heaven set your eyes
On my loving parents too;
Let me each day as I rise
Joyfully give thanks to you. Amen

LENTEN PRETZELS

The pretzel developed in the fifth century when Christians fasted from dairy products. These pretzels were shaped like arms crossed in prayer, because many early Christians prayed by crossing their arms over their breasts. Thus the pretzel is a sign of prayer and the cross. As you prepare to celebrate the triumph of the cross, use this recipe to make pretzels. Then, share them with friends, relatives, or homebound persons in your church community.

Add 1 tablespoon honey to 1½ cups lukewarm water (about 100° F.). Sprinkle in one envelope of active dry yeast and stir until dissolved. Add 1 teaspoon salt, blend in 4 cups flour and knead the dough until smooth. Divide the dough into six parts, roll each one into a 16- to 18-inch rope and then twist into a pretzel shape. Place the pretzels on a lightly greased cookie sheet. Brush with beaten egg and sprinkle with coarse salt. Bake at 425° for 12–15 minutes, until the pretzels are golden brown.

The Fifth Week in Lent

I am the resurrection and the life.

JOHN 11:25

Lazarus. The name reminds us of a truth we are always in danger of losing. Lazarus is a token of life in the midst of death, a token of the resurrection life, brought among us by God through Christ.

Alexander Schmemann, a teacher of many Christians in this century, wrote, "Christianity is not reconciliation with death. It is the revelation of death, and it reveals death because it is the revelation of Life. Christ is this Life. And only if Christ is Life is death what Christianity proclaims it to be, namely the enemy to be destroyed and not a 'mystery' to be explained" (*For the Life of the World: Sacraments & Orthodoxy* [Crestwood, NY: St. Vladimir's Seminary Press, 1973], 99).

Wherever Christ went in his ministry, death was revealed exactly because life was revealed. In the healings, in the parables, in his mission and ministry, Jesus exposes death as an enemy of God. This is never more clear than in the story of Lazarus, where Jesus challenged the normalcy and inevitability of death.

Lazarus died again, of that we may be sure. But the raising of Lazarus is a sign of God's compassion and a reminder of the raising of all people, indeed the raising of the whole creation (see Romans 8).

Our own resurrection from the dead is foretold and sealed in our baptism. In baptism we are buried with Christ into a death like his in order that we might know the joy of his resurrection. In baptism we join all those who have been made part of the resurrected and living body of Christ—just like Lazarus.

I called through your door,
"The mystics are gathering
in the street. Come out!"
"Leave me alone.
I'm sick."

"I don't care if you're dead!
Jesus is here, and he wants
to resurrect somebody!"

JELALUDDIN RUMI

HYMN

Precious Lord, take my hand,
lead me on, let me stand,
I am tired, I am weak, I am worn.
Through the storm, through the night,
lead me on to the light,
take my hand, precious Lord, lead me home.

Tune: PRECIOUS LORD

FOR READING THROUGHOUT THE WEEK

Ezekiel 37:1–14	John 11:1–45
Jeremiah 31:31–34	John 12:20–33
Isaiah 43:16–21	John 12:1–8

A PRAYER FOR THE WEEK

O God,
with you there is steadfast love
and the power to save us from final darkness.
May we live as servants of your mercy
and children of your gracious light. Amen

TABLE PRAYER

Through your goodness, O God,
you have blessed us with the gifts of this table.
Enlighten us with your grace,
and turn our hearts toward all those in need.
May our Lenten journey bring us to the rebirth of Easter. Amen

PRAYER WITH CHILDREN

I want Jesus to walk with me;
I want Jesus to walk with me;
all along my pilgrim journey,
I want Jesus to walk with me.

SIGNS OF NEW LIFE

Throughout the Lenten season, Ukrainian Christian women decorate the eggs which will be used in the celebration of Easter. After a short prayer, they begin to color the eggs with traditional symbols—spirals, triangles, suns, doves, trees. The eggs are given away as gifts to family members and friends. Many Christians see eggs as a sign of Christ's death and resurrection: when the hard, tomb-like shell is cracked open, the Easter colors of bright yellow and white spill forth. Use these days in Lent to decorate eggs for Easter. Create your own designs with water colors, dyes, or felt-tip markers.

HOLY WEEK

He humbled himself and became obedient to the point of death—
even death on a cross.
Therefore God also highly exalted him
and gave him the name that is above every name.

PHILIPPIANS 2:8-9

Sunday of the Passion / Palm Sunday

Blessed is the one who comes in the name of the Lord.
MATTHEW 21:9

This day is like a door. As it opens outward, there is joy and singing and loud exultation. Jesus comes in, amidst cheering and applause. Many churches hold a procession led by the children, with palms held high and mirth all about.

When the door closes, we see that Jesus must now remain, locked inside the room of his final week, where the singing will turn to silence and the cheers to shouts of "Crucify him!" German pastor and theologian Dietrich Bonhoeffer said, "When Christ calls a man, he bids him come and die." Our Lord issues that call because he first was willing to die. And that is what this day, really, is all about. Across all the shouting and jubilation falls the shadow of the crucified Lord.

That shadow may seem to ruin the party, to squelch the fun. Our joy is now tempered by the contemplation of the coming events of this most holy week. But if that gives us pause, it may be the perfect opportunity to recognize the truth as we turn from the palms to the passion. For that is how it was, and that is how it is: The accolades die away. The cross beckons.

And yet, the triumph remains for those who have eyes to see. Jesus suffers his passion trusting in God and faithful to his mission. The gospels portray him—rather than fate or political powers—in command. Jesus gives up his life on our behalf, it is not taken from him. He remains the king who reigns from the tree, that place where the human tendency to use power over others is turned upside down. Jesus' power is the desire to be with and serve those in need.

Ride on, King Jesus! No man can a-hinder me.
I was but young when I begun,
but now my race is almost done.
Ride on, King Jesus! No man can a-hinder me.
King Jesus rides a milk-white horse,
The river o' Jordan he did cross.
Ride on, King Jesus! No man can a-hinder me.

AFRICAN AMERICAN SPIRITUAL

HYMN

Refrain
All glory, laud, and honor to you, redeemer, king,
to whom the lips of children made sweet hosannas ring.

The multitude of pilgrims
with palms before you went.
Our praise and prayer and anthems
before you we present. *Refrain*

To you, before your Passion,
they sang their hymns of praise.
To you, now high exalted,
our melody we raise. *Refrain*

Tune: VALET WILL ICH DIR GEBEN

FOR READING THROUGHOUT THE WEEK

Monday:	Isaiah 42:1–9	John 12:1–11
Tuesday:	Isaiah 49:1–7	John 12:20–36
Wednesday:	Isaiah 50:4–9	John 13:22–32

BLESSING OF PALMS

*Use this blessing when placing palms in the home
after Palm Sunday worship.*

God of our salvation,
blessed is the one who comes in the name of the Lord.
Let this palm branch be for us a sign of Christ's victory
and our participation in the saving events of this great and holy week.
In our suffering give us faith and courage,
that dying and rising with Christ,
we may enter into the fullness of his glory. Amen

A PRAYER FOR THE WEEK

Lord Jesus Christ,
come to us in the power of your Spirit
and prepare our hearts to celebrate the great and holy days. Amen

TABLE PRAYER

Faithful God,
we glory in the cross of Christ.
With this food
nourish us for our journey from death to life,
and bring us to the joy of the resurrection,
through Christ our Lord. Amen

PRAYER WITH CHILDREN

Use this prayer responsively.

Holy God! *Holy God!*
Holy and Mighty! *Holy and Mighty!*
Holy Immortal One! *Holy Immortal One!*
Have mercy upon us. *Have mercy upon us.*

SPRING CLEANING

During this week, open the windows, shake the rugs outside, clean out the dustiness of the winter months from the top of your dwelling to the bottom. The guest of Easter is approaching and deserves our finest preparation and welcome.

Maundy Thursday

I give you a new commandment, that you love one another.
By this everyone will know that you are my disciples.

JOHN 13:34, 35

The Christian way is expressed in a short saying of Jesus: Whoever will lose his or her life for my sake will find it. Everything in Jesus' life testifies to this truth. During Lent we have rehearsed this truth in various ways, relearning it as we relive our baptism. We marvel at how this truth turns the customary truths of our world upside down.

Often we grasp after our own lives, clinging to them, holding them in place where they are. To this clinging comes Jesus, urging us to unlock our fingers, our minds, our hearts, and learn a new way. In the breaking of the bread, in the drinking of the wine, we see this truth: in the losing of life, we find our true lives in Christ.

We are called to a life of service, in which we discover who we really are by emptying ourselves out for others. In this we imitate Christ, who emptied himself, even giving up his life, for us. In following him, we hold onto this promise: as we are emptied, we will be filled; as we die, we will live.

This is the great mystery we have been learning and celebrating throughout Lent. It is the mystery that we celebrate today in bread and wine and in the washing of feet. It is the mystery we will celebrate tomorrow at the foot of the cross. It is the mystery of our new life, born of Christ's death.

So I may gain thy death, my life I'll give.
(My life's thy death, and in thy death I live.)
Or else, my life, I'll hide thee in his grave,
By three days' loss eternally to save.

RICHARD CRASHAW

HYMN

O Jesus, joy of loving hearts,
the fount of life, the light of all:
from ev'ry bliss that earth imparts
we turn, unfilled, to hear your call.

We taste you, everliving bread,
and long to feast upon you still;
we drink of you, the fountainhead;
our thirsting souls from you we fill.

O Jesus, ever with us stay!
Make all our moments fair and bright!
Oh, chase the night of sin away!
Shed o'er the world your holy light.

Tune: WALTON—*other tunes are noted in the index*

FOR READING THIS DAY

Exodus 12:1–14   Psalm 116
1 Corinthians 11:23–26   John 13:1–17, 31–35

A PRAYER FOR THE DAY

Lord God,
in a wonderful sacrament
you have left us a memorial of your suffering and death.
May this sacrament of your body and blood so work in us
that the way we live will proclaim the redemption you have brought;
for you live and reign with the Father and the Holy Spirit,
one God, now and forever. Amen

A PRAYER FOR FORGIVENESS

*The Jesus Prayer of the Orthodox Christian tradition is prayed silently
or out loud, slowly, repeatedly, and with the rhythm of the breath. It is a
simple prayer that can be spoken quietly or within the heart throughout
these holy days.*

Lord Jesus Christ, Son of the living God, have mercy on me, a sinner.

TABLE PRAYER

O Christ, the lamb of God,
by your passion, death, and resurrection,
you have brought salvation to the world.
Receive our thankful praise
as we gather at this table
and nourish us on our paschal journey
from death to eternal life.
You live and reign for ever and ever. Amen

PRAYER WITH CHILDREN

Use this prayer at bedtime.

Guide us waking, O Lord,
and guard us sleeping;
that awake we may watch with Christ
and asleep we may rest in peace. Amen

HOT CROSS BUNS

In England it has long been a tradition to eat hot cross buns on Good Friday. Prepare them the day before, to preserve the quietness of Good Friday.

To a recipe for basic roll dough, add ½ teaspoon cinnamon and ½ cup raisins or currants. Let rise. After rising, shape the dough into 2½" round buns. Place them on a greased cookie sheet about 1" apart; cover with a towel; let rise in a warm place for about 30 minutes. Bake at 375° for 15–20 minutes. Cool on racks. When cooled, draw a cross on the top by squeezing a frosting made of 1 cup powdered sugar and 1 tablespoon milk out of a snipped corner of a sandwich bag.

Good Friday

Upon him was the punishment that made us whole,
and by his bruises we are healed.

ISAIAH 53:5

We know all the right words. We know how to say, with the apostle Paul, the words, "while we still were sinners Christ died for us." But on this day, we stand in awe at the mystery of our salvation. The eternal enters the realm of time, the One who cannot die undergoes death. The unfathomable gift is before us as "it is finished"—it is complete.

Long ago, Christians who contemplated the meaning of Jesus Christ came up with the saying "what is not assumed cannot be saved." Human experience—from birth through death, all of the dancing and the dying, the singing and the sighing, the joy and the sorrow, the passion and the prayer—all had to be taken up into God so that the whole of human being and becoming would be restored to grace.

We are marked by the cross at baptism, and that mark is a sign that we are restored in Christ through the grace of God. All that we are, all that we shall ever be, is assumed into God on the cross.

Sin, of course, maintains its hold on us. Though Christ's cross-won victory is complete, we live in the in-between times, before the final showing-forth of that victory. And so sometimes it will not seem as though we have been taken up into God. We may even look around, seeking some new messiah.

But the cross remains before our closing eyes. The victory is ours, won by Christ's death while we still were sinners.

At the cry of the first bird
They began to crucify Thee, O Swan!
Never shall lament cease because of that.
It was like the parting of day from night.

Ah, sore was the suffering borne
By the body of Mary's Son,
But sorer still to Him was the grief
Which for His sake
Came upon His Mother.

THE SPECKLED BOOK

HYMN

What wondrous love is this, O my soul, O my soul!
What wondrous love is this, O my soul!
What wondrous love is this that caused the Lord of bliss
to bear the dreadful curse for my soul, for my soul,
to bear the dreadful curse for my soul?

To God and to the Lamb I will sing, I will sing;
to God and to the Lamb I will sing;
to God and to the Lamb, who is the great I Am,
while millions join the theme, I will sing, I will sing,
while millions join the theme, I will sing.

Tune: WONDROUS LOVE

FOR READING THIS DAY

Isaiah 52:13—53:12   Psalm 22
Hebrews 10:16–25   John 18:1—19:42

A PRAYER FOR THE DAY

Rejoice, O life-bearing Cross,
the invincible trophy of godliness,
the door of paradise,
the foundation of the faithful,
the protection guarding the church,
by which corruption is utterly destroyed
and the power of death swallowed up
and we are exalted to heaven from earth.
The invincible weapon,
the adversary of demons,
the glory of the martyrs,
the true beauty of the saints,
the haven of salvation
which gives mercy to the world.
By your cross, Lord Jesus,
you have brought life to the world. Amen

TABLE PRAYER

O Christ, the lamb of God,
by your passion, death, and resurrection,
you have brought salvation to the world.
Receive our thankful praise
as we gather at this table
and nourish us on our paschal journey
from death to eternal life.
You live and reign for ever and ever. Amen

PRAYER WITH CHILDREN

Here is a prayer to teach children as they trace a small cross first on the forehead, then the lips, and finally over the heart.

May the love of Christ
be in my thoughts (✛),
on my lips (✛),
and in my heart (✛). Amen

A DAY OF SILENCE

If possible, take the day off from work. Leave radios, televisions, and stereos off. Eat simply, perhaps a meal of soup and hot cross buns. Use this day as a time for quiet activity, prayer, and worship.

Holy Saturday

This is the night in which Christ breaks the chains of death
and rises in triumph.
O night truly blessed in which heaven and earth are joined.

THE EASTER PROCLAMATION

Tonight is different from all other nights because in the rhythm of the church year, tonight is the night of our incorporation into God, through that gift called the resurrection. Tonight the liturgy is our life; all the rest is commentary.

In this special night unlike all other nights, God emerges from the density of concepts, the thicket of ideas and doctrines. God comes, and God acts, and God becomes known in story and in movement and in the light which is Christ.

We come to the font of baptism, to that place where we first entered the reign of God, where the body of Christ included us, and where we were made at peace with God. In the waters of baptism our condition as strangers is washed away; we become a new humanity brought forth out of all the nations of the earth. We renounce the sway which evil and darkness has upon us and we lay claim to the God who has claimed us.

At last, we engage in that act which is truly our own as Christians. We join in the great and eternal thanksgiving, our offering of prayer, praise, and ourselves in service to the One who rescued us and brought us into the reign of God. We feast at the banquet of the Risen Lord. This act of praise is our calling, our duty, and our delight in this most holy of all nights.

Tonight the liturgy imprints us with the image of the crucified and risen Lord; all the rest of life is faithful living.

Hard it is, very hard,
To travel up the slow and stony road
To Calvary, to redeem mankind; far better
To make but one resplendent miracle,
Lean through the cloud, lift the right hand of power
And with a sudden lightning smite the world perfect.
Yet this was not God's way, Who had the power,
But set it by, choosing the cross, the thorn,
The sorrowful wounds. Something there is, perhaps,
That power destroys in passing, something supreme,
To whose great value in the eyes of God
That cross, that thorn, and those five wounds bear witness.

DOROTHY L. SAYERS

HYMN

There in God's garden stands the Tree of Wisdom,
whose leaves hold forth the healing of the nations:
Tree of all knowledge, Tree of all compassion, Tree of all beauty.

Its name is Jesus, name that says, "Our Savior!"
There on its branches see the scars of suff'ring;
see where the tendrils of our human selfhood feed on its lifeblood.

Thorns not its own are tangled in its foliage;
our greed has starved it, our despite has choked it.
Yet, look! it lives! Its grief has not destroyed it nor fire consumed it.

Tune: SHADES MOUNTAIN—*other tunes are listed in the index*

FOR READING THIS DAY

Genesis 1:1—2:4   Exodus 14:10–31
Romans 6:3–11   Matthew 28:1–10

A PRAYER FOR THE DAY

God of new life,
through our baptism into Christ you have raised us with him
to the joy of the resurrection.
You have brought us through the Red Sea
and fed us with the food and drink of the promised land.
May the fire of your love renew our faith
and deepen our commitment to you,
that we might faithfully live in the covenant of our baptism,
through Christ our Lord. Amen

EASTER THANKSGIVING FOR BAPTISM

*Use this prayer as you gather by a lighted candle
set next to a bowl of water.*

Gracious God,
we praise you for the new life you have given us in baptism.
We thank you for the bread of life
and cup of salvation that nourish us.
Through the power of your Holy Spirit,
bless us and strengthen us in the household of faith
so that we may serve each other in peace.
Through the turning of the days
and the changing of the seasons,
hold us secure in your loving arms,
and by the light of the risen Christ
lead us at last into the presence of your unfading light.
Grant this through Jesus Christ, the resurrection and the life,
who lives and reigns with you and the Holy Spirit,
one God, now and forever. Amen

TABLE PRAYER

O Christ, the lamb of God,
by your passion, death, and resurrection,
you have brought salvation to the world.
Receive our thankful praise as we gather at this table,
and nourish us on our paschal journey from death to eternal life.
You live and reign for ever and ever. Amen

PRAYER WITH CHILDREN

Sing this song at bedtime.

All praise to thee, my God, this night
for all the blessings of the light.
Keep me, oh, keep me, King of kings,
beneath thine own almighty wings.

Oh, may my soul in thee repose,
and may sweet sleep mine eyelids close,
sleep that shall me more vig'rous make
to serve my God when I awake.

THE LIGHT OF CHRIST

To create your own Easter candle, decorate a white pillar candle with a cross, the Greek letters *alpha* (A) and *omega* (Ω), meaning "Christ is the beginning and the end," as well as other symbols related to Easter. Wax sheets, available from craft stores, paints, and straight pins are just a few of the materials available to decorate the candle. Then place five whole cloves or five small wax nails in the candle at the four endpoints and center of the cross with these words: By his wounds, holy and glorious, may Christ protect us and preserve us. Amen

If you attend an Easter Vigil service this evening, you can bring home a flame by lighting a votive candle or tea light from the paschal candle in the church and placing it in the bottom of a canning jar. This light can then be used to light your own Easter candle at home. Light the candle throughout the fifty days of Easter, keeping it in a prominent place. Let the light of Christ shine brightly in your home.

BLESSING OF THE EASTER CANDLE

Use this prayer when you light the candle.

May the light of Christ, rising in glory,
dispel the darkness of our hearts and minds. Amen

Easter

Do not be afraid;
I know that you are looking for Jesus who was crucified.
He is not here; for he has been raised, as he said.
MATTHEW 28:5, 6

Easter Sunday

This is the day the Lord has made;
let us rejoice and be glad, alleluia.

PSALM 118:24

Easter is the feast of feasts, yet even in its splendor it doesn't stand alone. It is the culmination of Jesus' passion which led through the cross. The crucifixion seemed to be a dark time, the moment of Christ's defeat. In truth, it was the beginning of the victory. Just as Evil thought it had Christ in its clutches for once and for all, the image turns upside down, and Christ emerges as victor. The Evil One who by a tree once overcame, that ancient mythic tree from the garden of Eden where we fell in Adam and Eve, is now by the tree of the cross overcome. Only through the cross are we enabled to move to the joy of resurrection.

The Eastern Orthodox liturgy for Easter provides us with a powerful image on this day: Christ is risen from the dead, trampling down death by death, and bestowing life on those in the tombs. Think of that: "trampling down death by death." By his death Christ has destroyed death, and by his rising to life he has brought renewed life to all the faithful.

The traditional icon of the resurrection is an extraordinary image. Christ is depicted as rising from the tomb victorious; the grave covers are smashed and askew. Christ is reaching down into the darkness of chaos and death and he brings up the dead, beginning with Adam and Eve. From that darkness we, too, will be raised. O Happy Day! He is risen indeed! Alleluia!

Spring bursts today,
For Christ is risen and all the earth's at play.

Flash forth, thou sun,
The rain is over and gone, its work is done.

Winter is past,
Sweet spring is come at last, is come at last.

Bud, fig and vine,
Bud, olive, fat with fruit and oil, and wine.

Break forth this morn
In roses, thou but yesterday a thorn.

Uplift thy head,
O pure white lily through the winter dead.

Beside your dams
Leap and rejoice, you merry-making lambs.

All herds and flocks
Rejoice, all beasts of thickets and of rocks.

Sing, creatures, sing,
Angels and men and birds and everything...

CHRISTINA G. ROSSETTI

HYMN

> Come, you faithful, raise the strain of triumphant gladness!
> God has brought his Israel into joy from sadness,
> loosed from Pharaoh's bitter yoke Jacob's sons and daughters,
> led them with unmoistened foot through the Red Sea waters.
>
> 'Tis the spring of souls today: Christ has burst his prison,
> And from three days' sleep in death as a sun has risen;
> all the winter of our sins, long and dark, is flying
> from his light, to whom is giv'n laud and praise undying.

Tune: GAUDEAMUS PARITER

FOR READING THROUGHOUT THE WEEK

Acts 10:34–43   Psalm 118
1 Corinthians 15:1–11 John 20:1–18

A PRAYER FOR THE WEEK

> O God of the living and the dead,
> you have raised us with Christ
> from the water of baptism.
> We have died and our lives are hidden with Christ in you.
> Help us to live the baptism we have received with faith.
> Grant this through Christ our Lord. Amen

TABLE PRAYER

> O Lord, who has blessed five loaves in the desert,
> Graciously give us bread for life's needs.
> Almighty God, let not your gifts lead us into sin.
> Let not the goblet of sparkling wine induce us to misdeeds.
> While we enjoy our feast, let us also in charity remember
> All those who suffer want and hunger.
> May not the pleasure of the body stifle the inspirations
> of your Holy Spirit, O Lord. Amen

PRAYER WITH CHILDREN

The world reborn sings praises now,
the song ascends to green-leafed boughs.
So shout beneath the sunlit skies
to Christ who lives that we might rise!

WELCOME EASTER

Celebrate the resurrection throughout the entire day. Bring in fresh
flowers or blooming branches or whatever plant speaks of the seed
springing forth from the earth. Light the Easter candle. Put your best
cloth on your best table. Get out the rarely used plates or goblets or
whatever you have that is beautiful. The guest who comes this day is
the risen Christ, who receives the best that we have, whatever that
may be.

The Second Week of Easter

God has given us a new birth
through the resurrection of Jesus Christ.
1 PETER 1:3

We who have held our breath amid the wonders of Holy Week and Easter have finally exhaled. We resume ordinary breathing; life begins to look ordinary again. As the Easter Sunday festivities grow distant, we can think of this hymn:

> *Weary of all trumpeting, weary of all killing,*
> *weary of all songs that sing promise, non-fulfilling,*
> *we would raise, O Christ, one song: we would join in singing*
> *that great music pure and strong, wherewith heaven is ringing.*

Do we grow "weary of all trumpeting"? The victory is ours already—and not yet. We must still learn the song that is sung throughout heaven.

> *Captain Christ, O lowly Lord, Servant King, your dying*
> *bade us sheathe the foolish sword, bade us cease denying.*
> *Trumpet with your Spirit's breath through each height and hollow;*
> *Into your self-giving death, call us all to follow.*

Aha! So that's it. All the fuss, the feasting—all of it so that we might see that truth yet again: whoever wants to gain life must lose it. "Into your self-giving death, call us all to follow." For in that death is the life we so long for.

> *To the triumph of your cross summon all the living;*
> *summon us to live by loss, gaining all by giving.*
> *suffering all, that we may see triumph in surrender;*
> *leaving all, that we may be partners in your splendor.*

The triumph of the cross. This is the mystery at the heart of all our living. Let us pray for eyes to see it and the grace to embrace its mercy.

When will you ever, Peace, wild wooddove, shy wings shut,
Your round me roaming end, and under be my boughs?
When, when, Peace, will you, Peace? I'll not play hypocrite

To own my heart: I yield you do come sometimes; but
That piecemeal peace is poor peace. What pure peace allows
Alarms of wars, the daunting wars, the death of it?

O surely, reaving Peace, my Lord should leave in lieu
Some good! And so he does leave Patience exquisite,
That plumes to Peace thereafter. And when Peace here does house
He comes with work to do, he does not come to coo,
He comes to brood and sit.

GERARD MANLEY HOPKINS

HYMN

Jesus Christ is ris'n today, Alleluia!
Our triumphant holy day, Alleluia!
Who did once upon the cross, Alleluia!
Suffer to redeem our loss. Alleluia!

Hymns of praise then let us sing, Alleluia!
Unto Christ, our heav'nly king, Alleluia!
Who endured the cross and grave, Alleluia!
Sinners to redeem and save. Alleluia!

Tune: EASTER

FOR READING THROUGHOUT THE WEEK

Acts 2: 22–32	Psalm 16
1 Peter 1:3–91	John 1:1—2:2
Revelation 1:4–8	John 20:19–31

A PRAYER FOR THE WEEK

Risen Christ,
you come to us in your living word,
the sacraments of your love,
and the community of the baptized.
Open our eyes to see your presence. Amen

TABLE PRAYER

Come, Lord Jesus, be our guest;
let these gifts to us be blest.
Give the world your holy peace,
that all human strife may cease.

PRAYER WITH CHILDREN

Deep peace of the Running Wave to you.
Deep peace of the Flowing Air to you.
Deep peace of the Quiet Earth to you.
Deep peace of the Shining Stars to you.
Deep peace of the Son of Peace to you.

PRAYER AT DAWN

Dawn is generally a very peaceful time of the day. The earth is fresh from night and we are fresh from sleep. Try to arise before the sun rises at least one morning. Remember the dawn walk of the women to the tomb, and watch for the sun to rise. Bring your first thoughts of the day to God as you see the first rays of the sun in the east. You may use the following prayers or your own:

Jesus Christ is risen from the dead. Alleluia.
We are illumined by the brightness of his rising. Alleluia.
Death has no more dominion over us. Alleluia.

The Third Week of Easter

You have been born anew,
not of perishable but of imperishable seed.

1 PETER 1:23

After the resurrection, Jesus appeared to his disciples to make the point that his living presence among them had not come to an end. When we speculate about the exact nature of the resurrection, we easily miss that point: Christ is alive.

We Christians, limited as we are by our human understanding, tend to break up the work of God in our world into more manageable chunks: Jesus Christ was born. He lived and ministered among us. He died. He was raised. He will come again. But in doing so, we obscure the majestic whole: the mystery that God has broken in upon us from another realm with a salvation prepared before the foundation of the world.

The whole event of Jesus, from birth through resurrection, is God's one act. On rare occasions, we glimpse that majestic vision out of the corner of our eye—and we respond only with shouts of praise.

The incident on the Emmaus Road is one such glimpse into the whole mystery. The risen Christ is known in and through the word, interpreted with an eye toward the fulfillment; he is known in the breaking of the bread and the outpoured wine—and then he vanishes, leaving behind the burning hearts of the disciples.

So he is known to us today. With Maximus the Confessor, an early Christian writer, we glimpse that "whoever penetrates beyond the cross and the tomb and finds himself initiated into the mystery of the resurrection learns the end for which God created everything." It is enough for a life.

He preached upon "Breadth" till it argued him narrow—
The Broad are too broad to define
And of "Truth" until it proclaimed him a liar—
The Truth never flaunted a Sign—

Simplicity fled from his counterfeit presence
As Gold the Pyrites would shun—
What confusion would cover the innocent Jesus
To meet so enabled a Man!

EMILY DICKINSON

HYMN

O God of life's great mystery,
we bring to you this hopeful plea:
give us faith's insight strong and keen,
the joyful sense of things unseen.

Through preaching of the living Word,
in sacramental water poured,
with eucharistic bread and wine,
bring us the gift of life divine.

Tune: CANNOCK—*other tunes are found in the index*

FOR READING THROUGHOUT THE WEEK

Acts 2:36–41	Luke 24:13–35
1 John 3:1–17	Luke 24:36–48
Revelation 5:11–14	John 21:1–19

A PRAYER FOR THE WEEK

Lord of peace,
you open the hearts of your disciples
to understand the scriptures.
Reveal yourself to us in your word
so that we may know your love and mercy. Amen

TABLE PRAYER

Be present at our table, Lord;
be here and ev'rywhere adored;
these mercies bless and grant that we
may feast in Paradise with thee. Amen

PRAYER WITH CHILDREN

Use this song-prayer at bedtime.

Abide with me, fast falls the eventide.
The darkness deepens; Lord, with me abide.
When other helpers fail and comforts flee,
Help of the helpless, oh, abide with me. Amen

AN EMMAUS WALK

Set aside time to take a simple walk outdoors at least once this week.
What are the signs of spring in your part of the world? Where do you
see parables of new life around you? Become aware of all the small
things that are bursting with new life and offer a prayer of
thanksgiving. Keep your eyes open for the presence of the risen Lord.

The Fourth Week of Easter

You have returned to the shepherd
and guardian of your souls.

1 PETER 2: 25

Near the beginning of the Gospel according to John, Jesus is
called "lamb of God, who takes away the sin of the world"—
an acclamation familiar to us from the communion service.
Later in that gospel, though, comes an astonishing reversal of images.
In chapter 10, Jesus is shown as the door to the sheepfold, guarding
the entry and putting his own life in peril so that thieves or wild
animals may not come in to steal God's sheep.

Then the image refocuses to reveal the shepherd who lays down
his life for the sheep. Jesus, the lamb for sacrifice, rises in triumph to
become the Shepherd of the church.

> At the lamb's high feast we sing praise to our victorious king,
> Who has washed us in the tide flowing from his pierced side.
> Praise we him, whose love divine gives his sacred blood for wine,
> Gives his body for the feast—Christ the victim, Christ the priest.

The call to be a shepherd does not stop with Jesus. In John 21,
Christ appears to Peter and asks, "Do you love me?" In response to
Peter's affirmation, "Yes, Lord; you know that I love you," the risen
Christ says, "Feed my sheep." The sheep are to be fed in the
community of forgiveness that is the church. To this ministry of
feeding all of us are called through our baptism, through the gospel.
We sheep are called, through the power of Christ's resurrection, to be
shepherds of his flock.

Thunder entered her
And made no sound;
There entered the Shepherd of all,
And in her He became
The Lamb, bleating as He comes forth. Amen

EPHREM THE SYRIAN

HYMN

Savior, like a shepherd lead us; much we need your tender care.
In your pleasant pastures feed us, for our use your fold prepare.
Blessed Jesus, blessed Jesus, you have bought us; we are yours.

We are yours; in love befriend us, be the guardian of our way;
keep your flock, from sin defend us, seek us when we go astray.
Blessed Jesus, blessed Jesus, hear us children when we pray.

Tune: HER VIL TIES—*other tunes are listed in the index*

FOR READING THROUGHOUT THE WEEK

1 Peter 2:19–25	John 10:1–10
1 John 3:16–24	John 10:11–18
Revelation 7:9–17	John 10:22–30

A PRAYER FOR THE WEEK

Good Shepherd,
guide us with your word,
refresh us with the waters of life,
and strengthen us with your bread and overflowing cup. Amen

TABLE PRAYER

Lord Jesus,
you prepare a table before us
and feed us with the land's good gifts.
Strengthen us with food and drink
and lead us at last to dwell in the house of the LORD. Amen

PRAYER WITH CHILDREN

Jesus, tender shepherd, hear me;
bless your little lamb tonight;
through the darkness please be near me;
keep me safe till morning light. Amen

EASTER LAMB CAKES

In Bohemia it is a longstanding Easter custom to make a sponge cake
in the shape of a lamb, spread it with icing, sprinkle it with coconut
and decorate it for a special sweet dessert. Special molds for the cake
are available in craft stores, or the cake can be cut from a rectangular,
yellow or white cake. On Malta, the tradition is to eat pastries called
figolla, small pastry pieces filled with marzipan and cut in the shape
of a lamb. A similar dessert could be made by rolling or spreading
marzipan between two squares of frozen puff pastry. Cut it into the
shape of a lamb, and follow baking directions on the package.

The Fifth Week of Easter

You are a chosen race, a royal priesthood,
a holy nation, God's own people.

1 PETER 2:9

Through our baptism, we are connected intimately to Christ. One of the pictures he used for this intimacy is the vine and the branches. We have an organic connection to Christ. We grow out of him who is the vine rooted in God. We are nourished through our connection with and to him, even as he is nourished by his connection to the Father. We are prepared for ministry through this connection—but we need always to live from Jesus the vine and not merely from our own resources.

Many years ago, the Quaker writer Elton Trueblood spoke of the danger in becoming a "cut blossom society," a society in which we were no longer connected to the sources of our nourishment. An individual, even a church, can become chopped off from the source of life. When that happens, the blossoms survive for a time but eventually they die because they are able no longer to draw sustenance from the source of their life.

When we substitute knowledge as possession for knowledge as communion, we cut ourselves off from the source. Knowledge as love, knowledge as communion, knowledge as relationship: these kinds of knowledge are present in Christ the vine and his disciples the branches.

This communion flows through us to others. Christ comes in love to others through us as we remain in communion with Christ. In this way, a new commandment—to love one another—guides our life in this Easter season, and always.

A fish cannot drown in water,
A bird does not fall in air,
In the fire of creation,
Gold doesn't vanish:
The fire brightens.
Each creature God made
Must live in its own true nature;
How could I resist my nature,
That lives for oneness with God?

MECHTHILD OF MAGDEBURG

HYMN

Like the murmur of the dove's song, like the challenge of her flight,
like the vigor of the wind's rush, like the new flame's eager might:
come, Holy Spirit, come.

To the members of Christ's body, to the branches of the vine,
to the Church in faith assembled, to our midst as gift and sign:
come, Holy Spirit, come.

With the healing of division, with the ceaseless voice of prayer,
with the power to love and witness, with the peace beyond compare:
come, Holy Spirit, come.

Tune: BRIDEGROOM

FOR READING THROUGHOUT THE WEEK

Acts 7:55–60	John 14:1–14
1 Peter 3:13–22	John 15:1–8
Revelation 21:1–6	John 14:23–29

A PRAYER FOR THE WEEK

Lord Jesus,
in the waters of baptism
you have made us a chosen race and a royal priesthood.
May we proclaim your gracious presence in word and deed. Amen

TABLE PRAYER

We offer you thanks, God our creator,
for the blessings of this season
in which we celebrate the rising of Christ,
the springtime of salvation.
We offer you thanks for this meal
which is your gift of life.
Bless us with strength and courage
so that we may serve you in love. Amen

PRAYER WITH CHILDREN

Use this prayer at bedtime.

Now I'm sleepy, go to bed,
Close my eyes, lay down my head;
Father, let your watchful eye
Guard the bed wherein I lie.

Grant that all my family
Safe within your hand may be,
And all people, small and large,
Keep under your sleepless charge.

Give the sick of heart repose;
Help the weeping eye to close;
God in heaven, in your sight,
Give us all a blessed night. Amen

WORKS OF LOVE

An Easter custom in some parts of Germany is to slip messages into blown eggs and give them to people. The messages are usually on small slips of paper and contain promises, such as washing the dishes, weeding the garden, making a visit, or baking cookies. Think of people to receive such message eggs: neighbors, family, elderly church members, those in the hospital.

The Sixth Week of Easter

I will ask the Father,
and he will you give you another Advocate.
JOHN 14:16

Jesus promised his followers, including us, that they would be given an Advocate. The Advocate, the Holy Spirit, is one who stands alongside us and supports us. Our Advocate is the one who brings us into all truth.

What is this truth? Reformer John Calvin said that it is simply this, that the world is the theater of God's glory, and that Christ is the hidden, secret life of this world.

Under the Advocate's tutelage, then, we discover the relief of no longer having to make ourselves real as we go along. We no longer have to believe in ourselves, which is a lovely idea but after all a very limited prospect. When the Advocate comes to us, he convinces us of the truth about sin: We are led to see that the idea that we can make ourselves real very well without God, thank you, is a crippling illusion. We are shown the reality of judgment, in which such illusions are exposed for what they truly are. And we are given the strengthening presence of Christ in our lives, making us real by returning us to God.

On the verge of the season of the Spirit, the Advocate, the circle of love which has reached from God to us returns to its source in order that we might be drawn to God. But on that journey, we who have benefited from the Advocate are called to be advocates as well. We are invited to support and teach others, that they may join that circle.

Holy Spirit,
giving life to all life,
moving all creatures,
root of all things,
washing them clean,
wiping out their mistakes,
healing their wounds,
you are our true life,
luminous, wonderful,
awakening the heart
from its ancient sleep.

HILDEGARD VON BINGEN

HYMN

Love divine, all loves excelling, joy of heav'n, to earth come down!
Fix in us thy humble dwelling, all thy faithful mercies crown.
Jesus, thou art all compassion, pure, unbounded love thou art;
visit us with thy salvation, enter ev'ry trembling heart.

Breathe, oh, breathe thy loving Spirit into ev'ry troubled breast;
let us all in thee inherit; let us find our promised rest.
Take away the love of sinning, Alpha and Omega be;
end of faith, as its beginning, set our hearts at liberty.

Tune: HYFRYDOL

FOR READING THROUGHOUT THE WEEK

Acts 17:22–31   John 14:15–21
1 Peter 3:13–22   John 15:9–17
1 John 5:1–6   John 5:1–9

A PRAYER FOR THE WEEK

Spirit of truth,
strengthen our hope,
help us to keep a clear conscience,
and give us peace in the face of adversity. Amen

TABLE PRAYER

Bless all who are members of this family,
from the rising of the sun
unto the going down of the same.
Of your goodness, give us;
with your love, inspire us;
by your spirit, guide us;
with your power, protect us;
in your mercy, receive us
now and always. Amen

PRAYER WITH CHILDREN

Use this prayer in the morning.

Day by day,
dear Lord, three things I pray:
To see thee more clearly,
Love thee more dearly,
Follow thee more nearly. Amen

POMEGRANATES AND FIRE

Pomegranates have long been associated with Easter, because when they are cut open, they seem to be bursting with life. Serve a pomegranate this week if you can find one, or serve another fruit that has many seeds (kiwi, strawberry, watermelon). Read the descriptions of the gifts of the Holy Spirit in 1 Corinthians 12:1–11 and Galatians 5:22–26. Which gift do you feel you most desire or need at this stage in your life? Light a red votive candle and pray for that gift.

Ascension Day

You will be my witnesses.

ACTS 1:8

Our faith is breathtakingly out of the ordinary. This is never more clear than when we come to festivals like the Ascension. This picture of Jesus' departure from his disciples is unique to the gospel of Luke and its companion book of Acts. What purpose does it serve?

In his Large Catechism, Martin Luther writes about the phrase "Our Father in heaven," that this Name demonstrates God's nearness to all the faithful. Luther reasons that, since heaven is everywhere God is and since God fills all the creation with majesty and glory, therefore to call upon the Father in heaven is actually to call upon the Father who is as near to us as our own breathing.

The Ascension tells us much the same thing. In Acts, Jesus draws near to the disciples in Spirit even as he is removed from their sight. What they now lack in vision will be made up for through the power of the Spirit, who will enliven and direct the mission of the church.

The Ascension is, in a sense, the beginning of the church because it signals the drawing near of God the Holy Spirit, who guides the church as Lord through word and sacraments. The baptized are not distant from Christ because he has "gone up with a shout" (Psalm 47); rather, as we hear the gospel proclamation and as we partake in the meal, we are greeted and sustained by the eternal Christ.

The hand is risen from the earth,
the sap risen, leaf come back to branch,
bird to nest crotch. Beans lift
their heads up in the row. The known
returns to be known again. Going
and coming back, it forms its curves,
a nerved ghostly anatomy in the air.

WENDELL BERRY

HYMN

At the name of Jesus ev'ry knee shall bow,
Ev'ry tongue confess him King of glory now.
'Tis the Father's pleasure we should call him Lord,
who from the beginning was the mighty Word.

Humbled for a season to receive a name
from the ranks of sinners unto whom he came,
faithfully he bore it spotless to the last;
brought it back victorious when from death he passed.

Bore it up triumphant with its human light,
through all ranks of creatures to the central height,
to the throne of Godhead, to the Father's breast;
filled it with the glory of that perfect rest.

Tune: KINGS WESTON

FOR READING THIS DAY

Acts 1:1–11	Psalm 47
Ephesians 1:15–23	Luke 24:44–53

A PRAYER FOR THE DAY

> Lord Jesus,
> send your Spirit upon us and your church
> so that we may continue to serve you in peace. Amen

TABLE PRAYER

> Feed, O God, your loving children;
> Comfort those with trouble ridden;
> Bless these gifts which you provide us,
> That we richly have before us,
> That they may for daily living
> Power, strength, and cheer be giving,
> Till at last we with the faithful
> Come unto your heav'nly table. Amen

PRAYER WITH CHILDREN

> God has gone up with a shout,
> the LORD with the sound of a trumpet.
> Sing praises to God, sing praises;
> sing praises to our King, sing praises.
> For God is the king of all the earth;
> sing praises with a psalm.
>
> see PSALM 47:5-7

DAY OF ROSES

Ascension Day has been called the day of roses, since Christ ascended during the days of blooming flowers. Red rose petals were often scattered on the church floors. Take roses to the sick, the lonely, the widowed, the home-bound, the elderly, or whoever will enjoy receiving an unexpected surprise.

The Seventh Week of Easter

Protect them in your name that you have given me,
so that they may be one, as we are one.

JOHN 17:11

Here are a few questions that do not always yield quick and easy answers. Who will walk with us on life's path? Who will help us see and do what God intends? Who will protect us? When our folly or ignorance influences us, who will keep us from going astray?

Baptism has made us one with Christ, one with his death and resurrection. Baptism also gives us the ears to hear his prayer. "Protect them in your name so that they may be one. Protect them from the evil one. Sanctify them in the truth." We are not left without a direction. The One who speaks the truth and knows the deepest truth of our lives, will lead us and guide us.

Mothering Spirit, nurt'ring one,
in arms of patience hold me close,
so that in faith I root and grow
until I flow'r, until I know.

JEAN JANZEN, based on Julian of Norwich

HYMN

Come, Almighty, to deliver;
let us all thy life receive;
suddenly return, and never,
nevermore thy temples leave.
Thee we would be always blessing,
serve thee as thy host above,
pray, and praise thee without ceasing,
glory in thy perfect love.

Finish then thy new creation,
pure and spotless let us be;
let us see thy great salvation
perfectly restored in thee!
Changed from glory into glory,
till in heav'n we take our place,
till we cast our crowns before thee,
lost in wonder, love, and praise!

Tune: HYFRYDOL

FOR READING THROUGHOUT THE WEEK

Acts 1:6–13	Psalm 97
1 Peter 4:12–14	1 John 5:9–13
Revelation 22:12–21	John:1–26

A PRAYER FOR THE WEEK

Spirit of the living God,
restore us, strengthen us,
and lead us in service to all in need.
Keep us in your truth and unite us in one hope. Amen

TABLE PRAYER

As you once revealed yourself
in the breaking of the bread, O risen Lord,
be with us now as we share this food and drink.
Enlighten us with your Spirit
so that our words and actions
may be signs of hope for all people. Amen

PRAYER WITH CHILDREN

Pray this prayer with palms opened, turned upward.

Holy Spirit, hear me,
friend from God above.
You are always with me,
fill my heart with love.

PREPARING FOR PENTECOST

Pentecost Eve is another "blessed night" like Christmas Eve and Easter Eve. Some people observe the European custom of climbing to the tops of hills or mountains in the spirit of prayer. Others prepare for Pentecost by decorating their homes with brightly colored flowers and greens. Pentecost is called the *Green Holyday* in Poland and the *Flower Feast* among the Ukrainians. Easter has matured to Pentecost just as spring has turned to summer.

The Day of Pentecost

Jesus said to them, Receive the Holy Spirit.
JOHN 20:22

So at last, we come to the Spirit, who leads us in all the truth. In the dewy rush of new faith, people sometimes mistake personal prayer and scripture study for the fullness of the church. It's understandable. The exhilaration of having found a faith that is sustaining sometimes makes one look too much to the finder, and not enough to the giver, of faith.

Be careful. Too much emphasis on your own faith and you will burn out. The seed, thinking itself to be self-sufficient, sends forth a shoot but promptly dies.

But it need not be so. We are drawn into a community where others speak our language. We are brought in through the water. We are washed in order that we might come to dinner, an assembly of our brothers and our sisters. At the table there is much sharing and conversation.

The church is necessary and essential to our faith. The resurrection demands a community for celebration. The resurrection is the impulse to mission. The risen Christ sends out the disciples to teach and to baptize, to gather the community.

For the fifty days of the Easter season the paschal candle has burned brightly. Now we return to ordinary time again, to live out the Spirit in our daily lives and in our family setting. We will be God's hidden messengers in a world which needs us but does not know its need. The community of Christ will sustain us because the community is Christ in the midst of us through the power of the Spirit.

The dove descending breaks the air
With flame of incandescent terror
Of which the tongues declare
The one discharge from sin and error.
The only hope, or else despair
    Lies in the choice of pyre or pyre—
    To be redeemed from fire by fire.

Who then devised the torment? Love.
Love is the unfamiliar Name
Behind the hands that wove
The intolerable shirt of flame
Which human power cannot remove.
    We only live, only suspire
    Consumed by either fire or fire.

T. S. ELIOT

HYMN

Come down, O Love divine;
seek thou this soul of mine
and visit it with thine own ardor glowing;
O Comforter, draw near;
within my heart appear
and kindle it, thy holy flame bestowing.

Oh, let it freely burn
till worldly passions turn
to dust and ashes in its heat consuming;
and let thy glorious light
shine ever on my sight,
and clothe me round, the while my path illuming.

Tune: DOWN AMPNEY

FOR READING THIS DAY

Numbers 11:24–30   Romans 8:22–27
Acts 2:1–21   John 20:19–23

A PRAYER FOR THE DAY

Come to us, Holy Spirit,
and be the source of life restored.
Send your rain upon our dusty lives.
Wash away our sin and folly.
Heal our worn and wounded spirits.
Ignite the fire of your love within our hearts.
Burn away the apathetic hold of our ancient enemy.
Loosen what is rigid within us
and guide us in safety to our final home. Amen

TABLE PRAYER

Praise God from whom all blessings flow;
Praise him, all creatures here below;
Praise him above, ye heav'nly host;
Praise Father, Son, and Holy Ghost. Amen

PRAYER WITH CHILDREN

Pray this prayer in the light of a burning candle.

The Sacred Three be over me,
the blessing of the Trinity:
the sun, the warmth, the heav'nly light,
the flame and fire that gleam so bright.

THE RED OF FIRE

The color red has been associated with Pentecost, because red is the color of fire, of blood, of passion. Bring red flowers into your home, like peonies (often called *Pfingstrosen,* Pentecost roses, in Germany), geraniums, tulips, or roses; or if you have a garden space or balcony, plant a red flower suited to your area outside. Hang red, gold, and silver streamers in branches or from an open window to catch the wind and flutter. Light smaller candles around your Easter candle. Make red desserts such as strawberry shortcake, rhubarb pie, cherry cobbler, or a simple bowl of ripe strawberries. And, if you wish to carry your celebration a day farther, make gingerbread on Pentecost Monday, as has been the custom in England.

Hymn Index

"Savior, when in dust to you" may be sung to SALZBURG ("Songs of thankfulness and praise") or ST. GEORGE3S, WINDSOR ("Come, you thankful people come").

"I heard the voice of Jesus say" may be sung to CAROL ("It Came Upon a Midnight Clear").

O Jesus, joy of loving hearts" may be sung to WOODWORTH ("Just as I am") or ERHALT UNS, HERR ("Lord, keep us steadfast in your word").

"There in God's garden" may be sung to HERZLIEBSTER JESU ("Ah, Holy Jesus").

"Savior, like a shepherd" may be sung to REGENT SQUARE ("Angels, from the realms of glory") or PICARDY ("Let all mortal flesh keep silence") or PRAISE, MY SOUL ("Praise, my soul, the king of heaven").

"Love divine, all loves excelling" may be sung to BEACH SPRING ("Lord, whose love in humble service") or CONVERSE ("What a friend we have in Jesus").

"Come, Almighty, to deliver" may be sung to BEACH SPRING ("Lord, whose love in humble service") or CONVERSE ("What a friend we have in Jesus").

Acknowledgements

Sometimes I wake
By George Macdonald; public domain.

Savior, when in dust to you
Text by Robert Grant; public domain.

Two things, dear God, we need
"Zwei Dinge, Herr"; public domain; tr. copyright © Susan Palo Cherwien.

A mighty fortress is our God
Text by Martin Luther; copyright © 1978 *Lutheran Book of Worship.*

We give you thanks
Text by Martin Luther, emended; copyright © 1978 *Lutheran Book of Worship.*

The same leaves over and over
"In Hardwood Groves" by Robert Frost; public domain.

Baptized in water
Text by Michael Saward. Text copyright © 1982 Hope Publishing Co., Carol Stream, IL 60188. All rights reserved. Used by permission.

Your red blossoms amid green leaves
"Mabel Osborne" from *Spoon River Anthology* by Edgar Lee Masters, originally published by The MacMillan Company. Used by permission from Ellen Cogne Masters.

I heard the voice of Jesus say
Text by Horatius Bonar; public domain.

Now the day is over
Text by Sabine Baring-Gould; public domain.

I met a seer
"The Book of Wisdom" by Stephen Crane; public domain.

Amazing grace, how sweet the sound
Text by John Newton; public domain.

We thank you, our creator
Text by Matthias Claudius; public domain.

Loving God, who gives us all things
"Lieber Gott, Kannst alles geben"; public domain; tr. copyright © Susan Palo Cherwien.

I called through your door
By Jelaluddin Rumi. From *The Essential Rumi* by Jelaluddin Rumi, translated by Coleman Barks with John Moyne (New York: HarperCollins, Inc., 1995). Used by permission of Coleman Barks.

Precious Lord, take my hand
Text by George N. Allen, adapted by Thomas A. Dorsey. Copyright © 1983 Unichappell Music, Inc. Copyright renewed. International copyright secured. All rights reserved. Used by permission of Hal Leonard Corp.

I want Jesus to walk with me
African American spiritual; public domain.,

Ride on, King Jesus!
African American spiritual; public domain.

All glory laud and honor
Text by Theodulph of Orleans; tr. John M. Neale; public domain.

Holy God!
Ancient Greek acclamation in the Reproaches of the Good Friday liturgy, the Roman Rite.

So I may gain thy death
"Matthew 16.25—Whosoever shall lose his life" by Richard Crashaw; public domain.

O Jesus, joy of loving hearts
Text attributed to Bernard of Clairvaux; tr. Ray Palmer; public domain.

Lord God, in a wonderful sacrament
Copyright © 1978 *Lutheran Book of Worship.*

Lord Jesus Christ, Son of the living God
Public domain.

Guide us waking, O Lord
Copyright © 1978 *Lutheran Book of Worship.*

At the cry of the first bird
Tr. Howard Mumford Jones, from *The Romanesque Lyric: Studies in Its Background and Development from Petronius to the Cambridge Songs, 50–1050* by Philip Schuyler Allen. Copyright © 1928 University of North Carolina Press. Used by permission.

What wondrous love is this
American folk hymn; public domain.

Rejoice, O life-bearing Cross
Exaltation of the cross from the Orthodox liturgy; public domain.

May the love of Christ
Public domain.

This is the night
From the Easter proclamation, emended; copyright © 1978 *Lutheran Book of Worship, Ministers Edition.*

Hard it is, very hard
By Dorothy Sayers from *The Devil to Pay,* copyright © 1939 Dorothy L. Sayers. Used by permission of the Estate of Dorothy L. Sayers and the Watkins/Loomis Agency.

There in God's garden
By Király Imre von Pécselyi, tr. Erik Routley. Copyright © 1976 Hinshaw Music, Inc., Chapel Hill, NC. Used by permission.

All praise to thee, my God
Text by Thomas Ken; public domain.

May the light of Christ
Copyright © 1978 *Lutheran Book of Worship, Ministers Edition.*

Spring bursts today
Text by Christina Rossetti, 1830–1894; public domain.

Come, you faithful, raise the strain
Text by John of Damascus; tr. John M. Neale; public domain.

O Lord, who has blessed five loaves
From *The Easter Book* by Father F.X. Weiser, S.J. Used by permission of The Society of Jesus of New England.

The world reborn sings praises now
"Die ganze Welt"; public domain; tr. copyright © Augsburg Fortress.

Weary of all trumpeting
Text by Martin Franzmann. Copyright © 1972 Chantry Music Press. Used by permission of Augsburg Fortress.

When will you ever, Peace
Text by Gerard Manley Hopkins; public domain.

Jesus Christ is ris'n today
Latin carol; public domain.

Come, Lord Jesus, be our guest
Attributed to Martin Luther, with additions.

Deep peace of the Running Wave to you
Scots Celtic prayer; public domain.

He preached upon "Breadth"
Text by Emily Dickinson; public domain

O God of life's great mystery
Text by Royce J. Scherf. Copyright © 1978 *Lutheran Book of Worship.*

Be present at our table, Lord
Attributed to John Cennick and John Wesley; public domain.

Abide with me, fast falls
Text by Henry F. Lyte; public domain.

At the lamb's high feast we sing
Seventeenth-century office hymn; tr. Robert Campbell; public domain.

Thunder entered her
Text by Ephrem the Syrian; tr. Sebastian Brock, Fellowship of St. Alban and St. Sergius. From liner notes, John Tavener, *Thunder Entered Her.* Virgin Classics Limited, London. Permission requested.

Savior, like a shepherd lead us
Text by Dorothy A. Thrupp; public domain.

Jesus, tender shepherd, hear me
Text by Mary L. Duncan; public domain.

A fish cannot drown in water
By Mechthild of Magdeburg; tr. Jane Hirshfield. Translation copyright ©1989 Jane Hirshfield. Used by permission.

Like the murmur of the dove's song
Text by Carl P. Daw, Jr. Copyright © 1982 Hope Publishing Co., Carol Stream, IL 60188. All rights reserved. Used by permission.

Now I'm sleepy, go to bed
"Müde bin ich"; public domain; tr. copyright © Susan Palo Cherwien.

Holy Spirit, giving life to all life
Text by Hildegard von Bingen. From *The Enlightened Heart* by Stephen Mitchell, copyright © 1989 Stephen Mitchell. Used by permission of HarperCollins Publishers, Inc.

Love divine, all loves excelling
Text by Charles Wesley; public domain.

Bless all who are members of this family
By Mildred Tengbom. From *Mealtime Prayers,* copyright © 1985 Mildred Tengbom. Used by permission.

Day by day, dear Lord
Text by Richard of Chichester; public domain.

The hand is risen from the earth
By Wendell Berry. From *Farming: A Handbook,* copyright © 1968 Wendell Berry. Used by permission of Harcourt Brace & Company.

At the name of Jesus
Text by Caroline M. Noel; public domain.

Feed, O God, your loving children
"Speis uns, Vater, deine Kinder"; public domain; tr. copyright © Susan Palo Cherwien.

Mothering Spirit, nurt'ring one
Text by Jean Janzen, based on Julian of Norwich. Copyright © 1991 Jean Janzen, Fresno, CA. Used by permission.

Come, Almighty, to deliver
Text by Charles Wesley; public domain.

The dove descending breaks the air
By T. S. Eliot. Excerpt from "Little Gidding" in *Four Quartets,* copyright © 1943 T.S. Eliot and renewed 1971 by Esme Valerie Eliot. Used by permission of Harcourt Brace & Company and Faber & Faber, Ltd.

Come down, O Love divine
Text by Bianco da Siena; tr. Richard Littledale; public domain.

Praise God from whom all blessings flow
Text by Thomas Ken; public domain.